Original title:
Wrapped in Winter Wool

Copyright © 2024 Creative Arts Management OÜ
All rights reserved.

Author: Vivienne Beaumont
ISBN HARDBACK: 978-9916-94-398-4
ISBN PAPERBACK: 978-9916-94-399-1

The Velvet Grip of Winter's Touch

In cozy layers, I dress so quick,
My woolly socks are quite the trick.
A hat that's two sizes too large,
Makes me look like a fuzzy barge.

Snowflakes land with a gentle plop,
If I fall down, I might just stop.
With mittens thick, I try to wave,
But end up looking like a knave.

Dance of the Frigid Yarn

The needles click, a rhythmic beat,
I dance with yarn, though ice on my feet.
Each stitch I make is a wobbly cheer,
As I trip and fall, with no one near.

Laughter echoes, I can't deny,
My scarf's a mess that reaches the sky.
But in this fluff, I surely find,
A world where warmth and fun are aligned.

The Warm Embrace of Solstice

Hot cocoa spills; it's part of the plan,
With marshmallows floating like tiny men.
I wear my sweater, a riot of hues,
And dance like a fool while avoiding the blues.

The sun dips low, but I'm still a sight,
With my jammies on, I'm dressed for the night.
In cozy chaos, I feel so grand,
A winter warrior, in a playful land.

Tapestry of Cold Comfort

Furry blankets piled up so high,
Like a mountain where I almost cry.
Each layer thick, I can barely move,
But in this mess, I start to groove.

The fridge hums softly, a friend in need,
While I invent a snack no one will heed.
With giggles and crumbs, I take a stand,
In this chilly realm, oh, it's quite grand!

The Knit of the Night Sky

Stars twinkled like buttons bright,
On cozy sweaters, all a sight.
The moon was stitched with silver thread,
A giggle echoed, 'Time for bed!'

Knitting needles click and clack,
While squirrels sneak a midnight snack.
The chilly breeze tickles my nose,
As laughter dances through the froze.

A Tapestry of Frosted Dreams

In my dreams, a scarf so long,
It drags behind like a silly song.
Snowflakes float, they take a ride,
On tangled yarn, they slip and slide.

A mitten here, a hat out there,
With penguins posing without a care.
The frost creates a lovely mess,
But hey, it's winter, I must confess!

Garments of Frozen Memory

Old sweaters fight for space in drawers,
Each tells tales of winter wars.
A reindeer lost an antler, true,
While snowmen giggle in the blue.

Grandma's blanket, patchy and bright,
Holds secrets of our snowy nights.
With cocoa spills and laughter's flare,
We wore those laughs like we didn't care.

The Cozy Silence of Snowfall

Snowflakes whispered as they fell,
They wrapped the world in a chilly shell.
With little boots that stomp and squeak,
They made the quiet winter speak.

The shovels danced, a clumsy waltz,
While frost made hands feel like the faults.
And yet we giggled through the chill,
In frosty gear, we've had our fill.

Woolen Shadows Under the Moon

Under the moon, we dance with glee,
In sweaters thick as a bumblebee.
My hat's too small, it rides my brow,
A fashion statement? I wonder how!

The frosty breeze begins to tease,
I trip on my scarf, my knees the freeze.
Laundered dreams in woolly spins,
Each laugh erupts, a joyous din.

Frost-Embroidered Moments

In snowflakes soft, we slip and slide,
My knit mittens lost; I can't abide.
With each chilly gust, a chuckle grows,
I'll blame the dog for the frosty toes!

A snowman built with a lopsided grin,
His carrot nose? Oh, where to begin!
Three buttons down, and he's feeling proud,
But he can't dance in a raucous crowd.

Hearthside Hugs

By the fire, we roast our snacks,
One gooey s'more—then someone cracks.
The marshmallows sing and do a jig,
A sticky hand, oh what a gig!

Our woolly socks from head to toe,
But out they peek, oh what a show!
Tickling toes with laughter bright,
Who knew warmth could cause such fright?

Sanctuary in the Woolen Nest

Cuddled tight in our fuzzy lair,
The dog barks loud, and no one cares.
He rolls and snorts in a woolen heap,
As we all giggle and struggle to sleep.

Our blankets tease with a cozy chase,
And pillows thrown in a woolly race.
With laughter spilling, the night won't end,
A silly world where we pretend.

Shadows of a Sweater Night

In the crowded chair, I do sit,
The cat steals my warmth with a wit.
Yarn balls rolling, what a sight!
Who knew knitting could spark such delight?

Ghosts of fabric dance on the floor,
Twisting and turning, they ask for more.
With each stitch, laughter takes flight,
As we ponder, is this sweater too tight?

The Tender Threads of Winter

A scarf that's thicker than my dreams,
Pokes in all the silliest seams.
Each loop a giggle, each knot a tease,
Cuddle up, and you'll feel a breeze!

Hot cocoa spills, it all gets messy,
My mittens look quite a bit dressy.
But when I wave, they go awry,
Maybe hand-knitting's not my high.

Knit Together in Stillness

Two needles clash like swords in fun,
A battle lost, a victory spun.
As I fumble with loops in a tizzy,
My dog's on a quest for yarn that's dizzy!

In a world of patterns so absurd,
I mix my colors, oh how I blurred!
But in this chaos, joy is my bind,
Who knew creating could be this blind?

Embraced by the Arctic Breath

Frosty air makes my nose turn bright,
A hat too big, it's quite the sight.
I wobble about, like a penguin, you know,
Fashion sense lost in the wintery glow!

As snowflakes fall and snowmen rise,
My winter coat's a size too wise.
Each zip and tug a comedic fight,
Maybe spring is where I'll find my light!

Hibernation's Gentle Caress

When the sky shivers and sighs,
I wiggle my toes, like firefly spies.
The blanket holds me nice and tight,
Dreaming of snacks in the pale moonlight.

Cats are plotting an evening scheme,
While I realize I forgot to cream!
Hot cocoa spills on the brand-new rug,
As I giggle with all of the snuggly snug.

Textures of the Longest Night

Chunky knits and silly hats,
Warmth in a tangle, oh where are the mats?
Fuzzy socks in mismatched pairs,
Dance a jig in wooly flares.

A scarf that swallows me whole, oh my!
Wrapped like a burrito, I can barely fly.
Socks are monsters creeping at night,
But in this fluff, I'm ready for flight.

Serenity in a Woolen Embrace

With every stitch, I feel less cold,
Granny's yarn has a thousand tales told.
I stumble and trip in my oversized wear,
While fuzzy slippers float through the air.

The dog rolls over, all upside down,
In my chunky cardigan, I can't help but frown.
He's stolen my warmth and my cozy spot,
It's a wooly rebellion, and I've got naught!

A Lullaby of Wool and Snow

Snowflakes fall like lazy cats,
While I snuggle deep in fluffy hats.
The tea kettle whistles its happy tune,
As I dance around like a dish and spoon.

My mittens wave goodbye to the cold,
Telling stories of warmth and bold.
Woolly creatures start to jive,
As I chuckle at this cozy dive.

Wooly Respite Beneath the Stars

In hats so big, they wobble and sway,
A prance in the snow, we dance and play.
With socks of stripes, oh what a sight,
We giggle and slip in the moon's soft light.

The scarves are long, they drag behind,
A tangle of joy that we can't unwind.
Like sheep on parade, we frolic around,
In our cozy cocoon, where laughter's found.

A Veil of Icy Embrace

With mittens lost in an endless chase,
We juggle snowballs, what a funny race!
Frosty noses, all red and bright,
We chuckle aloud at our silly plight.

The chilly wind gives a cheeky nudge,
As we huddle close, not a single grudge.
Our breath forms clouds, like puffs of joy,
In a chilly world, we're the playful toys.

Sleepy Shadows of Soft Threads

In piles of fluff, we dive and roll,
These fuzzy layers warm every soul.
A snoring bear, or is it me?
We blend with the pillows, oh, what a spree!

Our cuddly kingdom, a fortress of knit,
Brought to life by every playful bit.
With dreams of cookies, we munch on air,
In this cozy huddle, we have not a care.

Cloaked in Winter's Whisper

A silken cloak of warmth we share,
In turtlenecks tight, with [ridiculous] flair.
Tickles abound, as we swap our styles,
The warmth radiates, sparking goofy smiles.

Through frosty trails, we strut and prance,
Our woolen garb leads a merry dance.
No fashion police, just giggles and cheer,
In this puffy haven, winter's fun is here.

Chasing Shadows with Warmth

In a coat so cozy, I prance and twirl,
Like a penguin in wool, giving winter a whirl.
Snowflakes tickle my nose, oh what a sight,
I laugh like a child, in the frosty light.

Mittens thick as pancakes, fingers all squished,
Chasing shadows of squirrels, my plans all brished.
With every slip and slide, my dignity's lost,
But who cares when warmth's paid the frost tax cost!

Snug Nestled in Winter's Hold

Snug as a bug in a blanket so tight,
I snack on hot cocoa, what pure delight.
Chasing my cat as she darts to and fro,
In a chase for the warmth, we weave to and fro.

The heater hums softly, a sweet winter tune,
As I plot mad schemes with a spoon and a moon.
A ruckus ensues, pillows go flying,
Each winter's adventure, my heart full of trying!

The Quietude of Woven Threads

A blanket made cozy with threads of great care,
I drape it around me like a fuzzy flair.
Knitting up chuckles, my yarn ball's a beast,
My cat tries to pounce, oh at least I have feast!

As needles click softly, the world melts away,
Each stitch a giggle, I'm losing my way.
With every loop twisted, I fashion a cheer,
In this quietude, I'll wrap up my year.

Home Beneath a Snowy Blanket

The world outside glistens, a quiet parade,
I snuggle in blankets, my perfect charade.
As snow drifts around like a fluffy dessert,
   I chuckle and revel in my cozy flirt.

The wind whispers secrets, but I hear my snack,
A stove full of goodies, there's no looking back.
With slippers like clouds, my footsteps feel light,
Home sweet home, where the laughter feels bright!

The Cloak of Chilly Nights

In a closet, I found my old gear,
It's a sight to behold, oh dear!
A jacket resembling a fluffy beast,
Ready for a cold night feast.

I put it on, it's two sizes too wide,
Waddling about, I took a pride.
Neighbors chuckle as I stroll past,
A sloth on a mission, but what a blast!

With pockets deep enough for a snack,
Who needs a gym when you've got this pack?
Every sneeze echoes, I fear I'll fall,
But this is the best cloak of all!

So pass the hot cocoa, let's have a cheer,
For the warmth, the laughter, the silly gear!
In layers of fluff, we tango and whirl,
Cold hands, warm hearts, it's a mad, fun swirl!

Whispers of Woolen Warmth

Warmth whispers secrets in thick, soft thread,
A knitted cat sweater, oh what have I wed?
With tails that tangle and sleeves that entwine,
My fashion's a riddle, refined yet benign.

When I step outside, I feel like a star,
Like I belong in a knitting bazaar.
Neighbors giggle, "Is that a live sheep?"
I bow with grace, then let out a beep!

The hat rolls down and covers my eyes,
I trip on the curb, oh what a surprise!
With every mistake, I'm a sight to behold,
Wrapped in a warmth that's wildly bold.

But laughter's the treasure, that's truly the key,
We tumble through snow, just you and me.
With jokes stitched tight in our cozy attire,
The whispers of wool set our hearts on fire!

Threads of White Silence

The snowflakes dance, a twinkling delight,
But I'm lost in a scarf three sizes too tight.
Gasping for air, a comedic refrain,
As I try to escape this wooly chain!

The dog gives a tug, I'm her newest toy,
In this fluffy ensemble, I'm not one to annoy.
With each yelp and bark, the neighbors all stare,
Just a wooly marshmallow—a sight beyond compare!

With mittens that clash and boots squeak when I walk,
I trip on my laces, oh how I squawk!
Yet in this white silence, bursts of laughter bloom,
A fashion faux pas that can light up a room.

So here in this winter, so cheerful and bright,
I prance with my pals, all wrapped up just right.
In threads of white silence, we share in this fun,
Stitching together, till the day is done!

Beneath the Icy Blanket

Beneath this frosty quilt, I take a leap,
In pajamas so puffy, I can hardly creep.
Like a marshmallow man, I wobble with glee,
Slipping and sliding—come, watch me spree!

Hot chocolate spills as I take my first sip,
Cocoa or snow? It's a fine line I trip!
My slippers are alien creatures with flair,
Creeping sideways like I'm in midair.

I dive for the couch, a slow-motion fall,
This icy adventure has me laughing for all.
With cushions behind and snacks on my lap,
The blanket jumps up—oh sweet winter trap!

So raise a warm mug to the silly and bright,
In the softest of layers, we hang on tight.
For under this icy blanket of dreams,
Laughter and warmth are the best of themes!

The Knitted Essence of Calm

In a sweater tight, just like a hug,
I dance and prance, but feel a tug.
My arms are stuck, like a bird in flight,
Playing hide and seek with sleeves of might.

A tangle of yarn, a playful mess,
My cat thinks it's a giant caress.
I roll and tumble, a playful game,
It's not just clothing; it's a claim to fame.

The Warm Hues of Winter Light

A scarf so bright, it glows and beams,
In colors bold, it sparks bright dreams.
I trip and stumble like a clumsy fool,
Who knew a scarf could be such a tool?

With mittens on, I wave goodbye,
To winter fun as I slip and fly.
A snowball fight, I take a stand,
But my gloves are soaked—oh, how unplanned!

A Haven of Loomed Warmth

Cozy blankets piled on high,
A fortress of fluff, where I can lie.
In this snug den, there's laughter and cheer,
As we sip cocoa, feeling no fear.

But wait! A dog claims my chair instead,
Now I'm on the floor, and he's in my bed.
A tug-of-war for the fluffiest space,
In the loomed warmth, we share this place.

The Stillness of Soft Sorrows

Beneath the weight of layers so warm,
I still feel small, like a tiny storm.
The warmth is there, but oh, the plight,
Why do my socks never match just right?

A cozy chair squeaks when I sit,
With my tea in hand, I'm one bit hit.
As snowflakes fall, I ponder and sigh,
Yet still, I giggle, as the minutes fly.

The Warmth of Handwoven Tales

In cozy nooks with threads of gold,
We share our tales, both new and old.
A tangled yarn, a snappy quip,
A stitch, a laugh, a playful slip.

The cat pounces on the yarn we toss,
While we're entangled, oh what a loss!
With every tug, our stories grow,
Who knew a ball could steal the show?

A tea that's steeped in friendship's cheer,
We sip and snicker, never fear.
For each warm hug and silly jest,
Knitting bonds that are truly blessed.

Beneath the Knitted Canopy

Underneath our cozy dome,
A fortress made, we call it home.
With colors bright and patterns wild,
We giggle as the winds grow mild.

The fluffy blankets play peek-a-boo,
While we tell secrets—oh, just a few!
A poke, a prod, a cheeky tease,
Our fortress shakes with fits of wheeze.

With woolly hats and scarves a-fly,
We march outside, all ready to try.
But trip we do, oh look—what fun!
Laughter echoes, the day is won.

Charmed by the Cold

Frosty air, we bundle tight,
In garb so bright, we bring the light.
Snowballs fly, our laughter rings,
With every toss, joy surely clings.

We slip and slide on icy ground,
A game of chase, some slips abound.
A frosty kiss turns cheeks to red,
But oh, the smiles—no tears are shed!

With woolly socks and mismatched gloves,
We strut about like graceful doves.
Embracing cold, we shrug and say,
In knitwear snug, we rule the day!

The Embrace of Evening's Chill

As twilight falls, the chill creeps near,
We gather close, with nothing to fear.
In cuddly coats and silly hats,
We share our quirks, like playful cats.

The fire crackles, popcorn pops,
Our jokes and jests never stop.
The night wraps round like a cozy quilt,
With every laugh, warm hearts are built.

Beneath the stars, our voices blend,
With craft and cheer, each moment we spend.
A tap on the shoulder, a giggle we share,
Under the chill, we haven't a care.

Warmth in the Stillness of Night

Cuddled tight, I snore with glee,
Hot cocoa dreams surround me.
Outside, the chill plays hide and seek,
While I seek warmth, so to speak.

Socks like clouds upon my feet,
My blanket fortress can't be beat.
Snowmen sneak an icy stare,
But I've no worries—I'm wrapped in care.

The Soft Embrace of Flurries.

Here comes the snow, it's quite a show,
A frosty dance with a chilly toe.
I step outside, slip, and trip,
What a sight, this snowy trip!

Snowflakes tickle my nose and chin,
Laughing loudly, that's how I win.
With mittens thick, I wave hello,
To frosty friends in a snowy glow.

Embrace of the Frosty Veil

Blanket of white, oh what a tease,
Every breath comes out as freeze.
My breath's a fog, a ghostly sight,
While hot soup warms my borrowed knight.

A snowball fight, oh what a blast,
Laughter erupts, we're having a blast.
The frost bites hard, but we don't care,
Frosty frolics fill the air.

Layers of Solitude.

Outside it's cold, but inside's a feast,
Three pairs of socks, I've turned to a beast.
With blankets piled high, what a sight,
A cozy kingdom in the night.

Pajamas on, I look like a blob,
This winter chill can't be a job.
With cookies and milk by the fire,
I hoard the warmth, my heart's desire.

Enfolded in Winter's Gentle Grasp

The snowflakes dance, a chilly prance,
A rabbit hops in woolly pants.
With mittens snug and noses red,
We laugh at all the warmth we've shed.

The sledding hill, a laugh-filled spree,
With wobbly boots, we sip hot tea.
But wait, what's that? A snowball flies!
A face full of frost, what a surprise!

The sweater's big, nearly a tent,
A fashion choice that leaves you bent.
Stuck in the armholes, oh dear me,
A cozy fit? More like a spree!

Yet through the chill, our hearts are light,
In woolly hugs, we take delight.
For in this frost, we find our cheer,
With laughter wrapped, we persevere!

A Woolen Whisper of Nostalgia

A hat that's knit, with pom-pom top,
We wear it proud, though it may flop.
The yarn's aglow, a vibrant sight,
But watch your head — it's quite a fright!

The mittens twirl, a tangled thread,
I tried to knit, but lost my head.
With patterns wild and colors bright,
My scarf could double as a kite!

A toasty hug, it fits just right,
Yet arms flail out, what a silly sight!
As we dance 'round, like clumsy bears,
We tumble down, forget our cares.

And as we sigh in frosty air,
A giggle hidden in our flair.
In woolen dreams, we take a stroll,
Unraveling joy, that's our goal!

The Cocoon of Frosty Bliss

In snowy realms, we take our flight,
A blizzard's song, a comical sight.
We slip and slide, our laughter loud,
In frosty bliss, we feel so proud.

Those layers thick, a blobby form,
In woolly suits, we brave the storm.
With cheeks so red and noses bright,
We waddle through the snowy night.

The cocoa warms, a sweet embrace,
With marshmallows adding to the grace.
But watch it spill, a chocolaty fight,
As we giggle, it's pure delight!

So here we sit, wrapped snug and tight,
Chasing snowflakes in delight.
With quirky hats upon our heads,
Our giggles echo where we tread!

Huddled Close Against the Cold

We huddle close, a giggly crew,
Wrapped in layers, our own zoo.
A scarf that's big, it's quite the feat,
Tripping over boots, feels like defeat!

Our noses red, yet smiles so wide,
As frosty winds become our guide.
A snowman built with eyes that wink,
But look! It's melting! Quick, don't blink!

The snowy streets, a thrilling race,
With sleds that glide and laughter's pace.
We tumble down, a snowy mess,
But underneath, pure happiness!

So when the chill bites with a grin,
We dance around, let the fun begin.
In woolen chaos, warmth we unfold,
The best of times, when it's cold!

Traces of Warmth Amidst the Chill

In the frosty air, noses glow,
Socks run amok, an odd little show.
Hats slide down to cover our eyes,
As scarves dance around with playful sighs.

Hot cocoa spills, a chocolate mess,
While snowflakes giggle, a glittering dress.
Slipping and sliding on icy paths,
Laughter erupts amid winter's laughs.

TOasty toes wiggle in their tight space,
As mittens unite in a fuzzy embrace.
The world wrapped in white, so slick, so sly,
With giggles and snowballs soaring high.

All bundled up, we march and cheer,
With rumbling tummies, festive and dear.
The chill can't stop our jolly parade,
In this winterland, memories are made.

Gentle Enfolding of Winter

A blanket of fluff hugs all it can,
Cats make snowmen—yes, that's the plan!
With skates on toes, we wobble around,
While frosty flakes do a twirling sound.

Mocha stains and marshmallow fluff,
Too much heat? Oh, that's quite enough!
We dip and dodge in our fuzzy coats,
Making snow angels, like joyful goats.

Puddles of laughter beneath frosty trees,
But oh! That branch? It's a slippery tease.
Snowballs whizz by, a flurry of glee,
As we trudge home, all messy as can be.

Winter lightly taps on our eager cheeks,
Whispers of warmth as the laughter peaks.
With red-nosed creatures and chilly delight,
We smirk and giggle, embracing the night.

The Wooly Heartbeat of January

Stitch by stitch, the yarns entwine,
A cozy dance, oh so divine.
Socks with holes, peers snicker and poke,
Yet warmth drips down with every cloak.

Puffing out cheeks, all snowed in tight,
Frosty noses bloom with rosy delight.
Pants befriended by chunks of dough,
As mitts and hats all stagger in tow.

Backyard squabbles and snowball fights,
Laughter charges through winter nights.
A knit cap pulled low, eyes peek out,
While dreams of spring turn into a stout.

In shivery chill, we summon our cheer,
As woolen monsters linger near.
Soft stitches weave stories, warm and bright,
Carrying us through the snowy night.

Embracing Shadows of Comfort

In the glow of lights, mismatched socks play,
Dancing around for a glorious display.
Chilly air greets our festive crowd,
We giggle at sweaters, all goofy and proud.

The misfit of mittens starts a debate,
One's missing finger makes us create.
We huddle for warmth, snug as can be,
Our giggles echo, a winter jubilee.

Like a marshmallow mishap in a cup,
Sipping hot drinks, we can't get enough.
A rooftop covered, like whipped cream's cap,
We tumble and tumble, fall in a flap.

As shadows stretch on cold winter lanes,
Woolly creatures dance, ignoring the rains.
With joy and warmth, we leap and we spin,
Amongst all the laughter, let the fun begin!

Tucked Beneath a Frosty Sky

Puffy clouds like marshmallows,
Tossed upon a blue delight.
Woolly hats and mittens snug,
Hopping 'round in frosty flight.

Snowflakes fall like sugar sprinkles,
On noses cold and cheeks so red.
Laughing loud, we roll and tumble,
Like penguins on a snowy bed.

Sleds go zooming down the hill,
With squeals and wobbly swoops of glee.
A snowman melts with a cheeky grin,
His carrot nose? A mystery.

Hot cocoa waits, a treat to share,
With marshmallows dancing high.
Gather 'round, let stories soar,
Beneath this frosty blanket sky.

The Embrace of Snug Solitude

Blankets piled like fluffy clouds,
Cocooned in layers, feeling grand.
Socks that match? Not even close!
A fashion choice both bold and bland.

Cuddled deep with cats galore,
Their purring sounds like winter's hum.
What's that smell? Oh, it's the stew!
Dinner's late? Well, here I come!

Worn-out shoes and fuzzy pants,
Who needs a mirror on display?
Sipping tea, I do a dance,
In my comfy, quirky way.

Outside, the world is freezing bright,
But in here, I reign supreme.
With whimsy in my woolly realm,
Living life, it's quite the dream!

Frosty Threads of Memory

Scarves that tell of seasons past,
With tales of mishaps, joy, and cheer.
A balmy hat from days gone by,
That swears it's always summer here.

Shovels, mittens, socks askew,
Pants tucked into ice skates tight.
Tumbling 'round, we laugh and fall,
In this wooly, wild delight.

Grandma's knit with love and care,
Worn until the fabric's thin.
Each stitch a giggle, each yarn a tear,
Echoes of the joy within.

Frosty mornings, warm inside,
Where memories meet the chilly air.
We twirl and swerve, on snowy streets,
In our wooly past, beyond compare.

Lofty Layers in a Chilly Breeze

Layered up, I look so weird,
Like an igloo on the go.
My nose so red, it has my peers,
Wondering if I'm part of snow.

Puffy jackets, mittens bright,
All my friends are decked like me.
We waddle, slip, and dance on ice,
Making winter's art spree.

Giggling hard, I trip and fall,
But up I pop with a snowball whack!
Woolly warmth and frosty fun,
Wrapped in layers, no turning back.

Chilly whispers in the air,
Encourage silly, swirly spins.
With each turn, the laughter grows,
In this frosty world, our joy begins.

Stitches Beneath the Stars

In the chill of the night, we cozy and snore,
With a sweater so tight, who needs a front door?
Socks mismatched, a sight to behold,
Dancing in wool, we're bright and bold.

The cat plops down, stealing our heat,
A regal throne of knitted retreat.
Needle clicks echo, like whispers of cheer,
While we sip hot cocoa, never fear!

Stitches and laughter, the fabric of fun,
With each little loop, our care has begun.
Tangled together, we share in the smiles,
As jokes fly around, warming our miles.

When the sun peeks out, and the frost begins to fade,
We'll unravel our tales, the wool that we made.
But till then, we'll snicker in our cozy embrace,
In these mismatched threads, we've found our place.

Knitted Echoes of Solstice

In the glow of the fire, we twiddle our thumbs,
With yarn flying high, like frolicking chums.
A scarf turns to a monster, it's giving us grins,
As we stitch up the laughter, let the fun begin!

We poke fun at knitting, what a messy affair,
A hat for the dog? Oh, dare we dare!
With needles a-clickin', and yarn on a spree,
Each error a story, that's delightful glee.

The winter winds howl, while we laugh in our nooks,
Sipping on hot tea, sharing funny books.
Each tangled yarn adds to the giggle parade,
In our knitted chaos, no fun will be made!

As the stars twinkle down, they join in our cheer,
For every stitch made, we hold laughter near.
So let the patterns dance, and the yarns intertwine,
In this knitted adventure, we all feel divine.

Frosted Dreams in Yarns

Under blankets we sit, soft as the snow,
While our knitting projects just won't let go!
Loops turning to tangles, it's a woolly fright,
Yet laughter's the thread, twinkling so bright.

With each silly faux pas, like hats on our heads,
We strut round the house, like proud little threads.
The cat thinks it's fun to unravel our care,
While we burst into giggles, no burden to bear.

A blanket of warmth wrapped snug like a hug,
Turns us into cookies, all cozy and snug.
Winter's harsh breath never leaves us in tears,
For we spin soft dreams, and snicker through fears.

So here's to our folly, and yarn mishaps grand,
Stitching up moments, side by side we stand.
With needles in hand, we banter and play,
In this frosted delight, come what may!

Cloaked in Subtle Warmth

When the world is icy, and nose hairs freeze,
We wear our best wool, like it's a grand tease.
Scarves that could double as hats for a bear,
Yet, in this absurdity, we don't have a care.

With yarn in our laps, we craft and we poke,
Each stitch a giggle, a whimsical joke.
The fire sings softly, a cozy tune hums,
As we huddle close, like two playful chums.

Buttons mismatched, and colors all wrong,
Remind us of silly times, where we belong.
With every old sweater, we remember the smiles,
Stitched into fabric, enhancing our styles.

So here's to the wool, that's too warm for the day,
To laughter and warmth, in this tangled ballet.
As we frolic in winter, in coats made of fun,
We'll knit our own stories, until the day's done!

Layers of Snow-Kissed Comfort

On icy days, I wear a hat,
It makes me look like a fluffy cat.
My scarf's a snake around my neck,
I trip on it—oh, what the heck!

The mittens are two fuzzy beasts,
I wave them 'round like furry feasts.
A coat that swallows me whole, my friend,
In this warmth, I never want to end.

When snowflakes dance on my big nose,
I laugh as I brave the winter's pose.
My toes are sausages in my boots,
But I smile, with silly, silly roots.

So here's to layers, goofy and fun,
Like wearing twenty animals, one by one.
In cozy confusion, I shall remain,
A jolly snowman, feeling no pain!

The Embrace of Frosty Fibers

I donned my sweater, two sizes too vast,
In its hug, I'm a fashion faux pas blast.
The sleeves could fit a hippo's round arms,
But I strut like a peacock, flaunting my charms.

My socks are mismatched, a colorful crew,
One's argyle, and one's a bright, silly blue.
They peek from my boots as I wiggle and dance,
Bringing smiles to folks in my woolly romance.

The earmuffs sit high, but one's slipping down,
For peak winter fun, I'm the silliest clown.
I twirl in the frosty air with delight,
Snug as a bug, all bundled up tight.

So in fuzzy fashion, I'll settle my claim,
Each winter attire, ridiculous fame.
For every misstep in this cold, joyous roam,
I wear my knitting with pride—this is home!

Weaving Warmth Against the Cold

A blanket of yarn thrown over my chair,
It catches my cat with a curious stare.
The cushions are piled, a fortress of knit,
With laughter and giggles, we cozy and sit.

The hot cocoa's bubbling, marshmallows collide,
I sip from a cup that's too big to hide.
My toes dive deep in this woolly delight,
Please no one interrupt this cozy, soft night.

The heater is on, but I'm layered and warm,
With jumpers that battle the cold's frosty charm.
I'll stand by the window, all snuggly and fat,
And wave to the neighbors—all dressed like a brat.

In the embrace of my makeshift retreat,
I'll share my warm cookies; come join me, let's eat!
For winter's a stage where we strut and we play,
In our knitted kingdom, we laugh through the day!

Where Cold Meets Cozy

The shivers are sneaky; they creep in my door,
But I bounce back with layers—who needs a chore?
I tumble and fumble, all cuddled in fluff,
Dancing like a chicken, feeling warm enough.

My balaclava's hugging my head way too tight,
It gives me the vision of a kangaroo's fright.
I waddle like penguin and trip on my gloves,
But all that I need is the warmth that I love.

The snowflakes are laughing, they tickle my nose,
With every fresh flurry, my joy overflows.
My cheeks are bright red, my fingers like ice,
Yet here with my humor, I'll never think twice.

So come join the fun in this wintery zone,
Where laughter's the fire warming each fluffy home.
In a world draped in comfort, we'll find our way through,
All bundled together, no matter the view!

Hearthbound Hearts

By the fire we sit and toast,
Socks that smell, they matter most.
Hot cocoa spills, oh what a sight,
Laughter dances in the night.

As the flames crackle and pop,
We share our secrets, let them drop.
Mismatched mittens, oh what a pair,
Creating warmth from frosty air.

Cranberry sauce on the cat's nose,
Funny stories, in giggles we doze.
Woolly hats with comfy seams,
Fuzzy dreams of silly memes.

Friends and family gathered near,
In cozy circles, strife disappears.
With every chuckle, we're snug and free,
Hearing holiday tunes off-key.

Enveloping the Frosted Air

Snowflakes swirl, a dance unique,
Chilly noses play hide and seek.
In the park, snowmen on parade,
With carrot noses, looking well-made.

Sleds and laughter, joy on the slide,
Hot soup spills when we take a ride.
Scarves become a tangled game,
Fashion faux pas? Oh, we're to blame!

Winter air, fresh as a sneeze,
Chasing friends among the trees.
Snowball fights with slushy aim,
Who knew winter could be a game?

Crisp evening walks, our cheeks aglow,
Tripping on ice, a comical show.
Slipping and sliding, oh what delight,
In shivery laughter, we take flight.

Knots of Comfort on Cold Days

Bundled tight in layers piled,
Outrageous knits, like a toddler styled.
Scarves that wrap from head to toe,
Fuzzy fashion's glorious show.

Puddles splash as we stomp through,
Wet socks squish with that squishy goo.
Mittens gone, just one on a hand,
Who knew winter would be so unplanned?

Sipping tea, with stories that loop,
Filling the room like a warm, cozy soup.
Cats in blankets, looking so sly,
As they watch us shuffle by and by.

Laughter rings like a jingle bell,
In every wrinkle, there's a tale to tell.
On cold days, we find our way,
Knots of comfort, come what may.

The Softness of Quietude

Snowflakes tumble, soft as pie,
Whispers of winter flutter by.
In our blankets, we snuggle tight,
Comfy chaos, pure delight.

Outside, the world is fresh and white,
While in, we munch with merry bite.
Pillow forts hide giggling glee,
In this cozy world, just you and me.

Hot chocolate spills, oops, what a scene,
Chocolate smiles, oh what a sheen!
In the stillness, we find our cheer,
In every moment, winter's dear.

With fuzzy slippers shuffling low,
We seek warmth in the afterglow.
Joy in simplicity fills the air,
In this silly snow, none can compare.

Threads of Solitude and Warmth

In layers piled high, I struggle to rise,
My outfit's a fortress, a woolly surprise.
I waddle like penguins, not built for sharp turns,
In this knit cocoon, a new humor I learn.

The cat thinks I'm fuzzy, a giant to tease,
Paws on my slippers, oh please, pretty please!
But clumsy I am, with yarn in a knot,
As I laugh at my jigsaw, a silly jackpot.

Like fashion gone mad at a style show of sheep,
I strut in my knits; it's a laugh, not a leap.
Each stitch holds a tale, a giggle or two,
As I spin into mischief, all cozy with you.

We dance in the fluff, it's a wobbly sight,
And share in the warmth, 'neath the big quilted light.
With coffee at hand and our socks mismatched,
In threads soft and silly, our laughter's attached.

Embracing the Silence of Snow

Snowflakes are stealing the spotlight today,
As I trudge through the drifts in a humorous way.
With boots big as boats, I'm sunk to my knees,
Embarrassed by snowmen, they stand with such ease.

The air's full of giggles, under a cloud,
Where snowballs are launched, and the kids cheer so loud.

But here in my scarf, like a burrito I'm wrapped,
With frost on my nose, oh how I've been zapped!

As I'm rolling and tumbling, I hear a soft crack,
It's the sound of my dignity, tumbling back.
Yet in this white wonder, with chuckles and cheer,
I find joy in the chaos; winter's so dear!

With snowmen as witnesses, we make a mad dash,
Through flurries and giggles, avoiding a crash.
So here's to the solace, the laughter, the play,
In a world full of white, let's just drift away!

Comfort in the Heart of Winter

The heater's a miracle, a roaring delight,
While I sip on my cocoa, all snug and tight.
A blanket of laughter, a pillow of cheer,
In the heart of this storm, love's warmth is so near.

The ice outside twinkles, a crystal ball game,
While we snuggle together, no need for a flame.
Our puns are like snowflakes, each one is unique,
As we chuckle through winter, no reason to freak!

Mittens and slippers, a fashion faux pas,
We strut with our hot drinks, we're hitting the spa!
But hey, who's to judge? In our cozy embrace,
With laughter unspooling, we're winning this race.

So let's toast to the weather, with blankets and fun,
In this frosty escapade, we've already won.
With each silly moment, we generate heat,
In a comfy cocoon, winter's ultimate treat!

A Tidal Wave of Woolen Warmth

Here comes the wool wave, a tsunami of fluff,
With scarves long as rivers, I'm feeling quite tough.
A sweater tsunami, like a woolen retreat,
With layers aplenty, I can't feel my feet.

Each time I bend over, it's a comedy show,
As I trip on my sweater; oh, where did it go?
More fabric than man, I'm bobbing like boats,
In this tidal embrace, with my woolen quotes.

I juggle my mittens, like clowns with their pies,
While snowflakes join in a theatrical rise.
With laughter contagious, my wool's gone awry,
Unraveling mischief, like clouds in the sky.

So let's dance in our layers, let absurdity reign,
In this woolly adventure, we'll smile through the rain.
With friends and our laughter, let's ride this warm wave,
For a chuckle in winter is the comfort we crave!

Cozy Threads of Frost

A squirrel in a sweater, how absurd,
He scampers and jumps, so undeterred.
His nutty stash tucked snug with glee,
In a woolly world, he's as cozy as can be.

Puffy mittens hug my hands tight,
In a snowball fight, I've lost all my might.
My nose is red, oh what a sight!
Who knew winter could be such a delight?

A hat with ears sits far on my head,
Like a furry mushroom, I feel well-fed.
Friends laugh at my clumsy, warm clomp,
In slippery shoes, I dance and I romp.

So here's to sweaters, knit with a cheer,
Bringing us laughter and jolly good cheer.
With every stitch, a giggle we weave,
In these thick threads, we truly believe.

Embracing the Chill

Fluffy socks peek from under the bed,
With a waddle, I walk, almost misled.
I trip on my own, who knew it was tough?
To hustle in layers, oh winter, enough!

Hot cocoa spills on my favorite scarf,
In my clumsy haste, I could hear one laugh.
Tiny marshmallows are dodging the chill,
While I'm in the kitchen, anxious for a thrill.

A penguin slide on the icy ground,
Consider me graceful as I tumble around.
I giggle and wiggle and wave to the crowd,
Like a bottle of soda, popping too loud!

So let's all embrace the winter's fun,
With giggles and tumbles, and frolics run.
In this frosty playground, we banish despair,
With fluffy mischief and laughter to share.

A Tapestry of Thaw

The snowman waves with a carrot nose,
While I'm stuck in a parka that endlessly grows.
I can barely see through my goggles so wide,
Oh winter, you're hilarious; just look at me slide!

Icicles hang like a dazzling display,
I pretend they're jewels, just for a play.
A hot cup of cheer spills on my lap,
But who cares, it's cozy, I'll just take a nap!

Snowflakes dance like confetti in air,
While I struggle not to lose my warm hair.
With fleece blankets tall and slippers galore,
Winter's mischief keeps us wanting more.

So let's build a fort, use cushions and chairs,
Tell tales of polar bears and winter affairs.
In this frosted laughter, we'll snuggle and stay,
Making memories in our own silly way.

Hearthside Whispers of December

The fire crackles with a pop and a hiss,
As I sip from my mug, oh, pure bliss!
A cat in a blanket, a king on his throne,
The winter's chill can't chill our cozy zone.

In slippers like boats, we sail through the room,
Stepping on squeaky toys that add to our gloom.
A snowball fight turns into a race,
As smiles and laughter take over the space.

The cookies are burned, I admit it's true,
But who cares when I've still got my crew?
We laugh 'til we cry, by the warm firelight,
In moments like these, everything's just right.

So gather around, with stories galore,
In this twist of winter, let laughter soar.
In the heart of December, in moments we keep,
We find warmth in joy, as we drift off to sleep.

The Comfort of Knitted Dreams

A hat that's two sizes too large,
Fuzzy strands fraying at the edges,
I wear it with pride, looking quite odd,
The laughter echoes from my three-legged dog.

Each mitten mismatched, a colorful sight,
One's for aliens, the other's for fright,
I snack on a cookie, it crumbles to dust,
In this woolly wonder, oh how I must trust.

A scarf that stretches from here to the moon,
A fashion statement? Maybe too soon,
My friends giggle loud when they come to visit,
In hand-knit chaos, who wouldn't feel blissed?

As toast pops up with a playful jolt,
It lands right in the yarn, a buttery vault,
In the land of whiffs and clanking mugs,
We revel in warmth and laugh at the shrugs.

Snug Embrace of the Dark Season

The blanket's so hefty, I shuffle and cling,
Couch hugs my body, it's quite a weird fling,
I trip on my woolly socks, what a fate,
Keep laughing, dear friends, I can't contemplate!

Pajamas adorned with funky designs,
Dancing in patterns that twist and entwine,
A chill in the air - oh what a delight,
We gather around to spill stories till night.

Tea spills on the floor in a whimsical pass,
As I wrangle a quilt made of teddy bear grass,
The rug's a giant knit that welcomes all feet,
While my cat in a ball gives a proud little bleat.

Beneath all this fuzz, what warmth do we find?
A poke of the elbow, a smile that's kind,
With laughter we cheer through the long, chilly spree,
In snug, silly dreams, we're all so carefree.

Tangles of Frostbitten Yarn

A basket of colors, a jumbled delight,
My needle's gone rogue, it's causing a fight,
It dances away with a gleeful escape,
As I chase down the yarn with a comical shape.

In the corner it hides, that yarn full of glee,
I swear it's conspiring to laugh at me,
Each stitch, a betrayal, a loop so unkind,
I whisper to it, help out, never mind!

A tangled mess grows, it's knitting mayhem,
Pulls at the laughter and the cheer—I can't stem,
The socks rise up, with a playful revolt,
Stripes and polka dots, oh what an insult!

I finally give in, embrace the great twist,
In frosty commotion, I find I can't resist,
For laughter erupts from my cozy abode,
As I promise my yarn, we'll share this fun road.

Cozy Corners of a Cold Hearth

The fire crackles, so merry and bright,
With marshmallows bouncing around in delight,
My mittens are singing their own silly song,
As we roast up the treats and cheer all night long.

The rug's a trampoline for kittens and glee,
As my old buddy Jack bursts with jokes over tea,
We sport our best sweaters, those hideous finds,
And dance in our shadows like colorful blinds.

Another warm drink spills—oh what a scene!
We laugh off the chaos while munching on beans,
The cup's an adventure, and what do we see?
We're all just knitters of joy by decree.

So we cozy it up, with a wink and a tease,
In corners we giggle, our laughter's the breeze,
With a tug at the collar and a stretch of the arm,
In this charming cold season, we all find our charm.

Fragments of a Frosty Evening

Snowflakes tumble, oh what a sight,
My nose is red, but I feel quite bright.
A penguin slips, a comic fall,
Laughter echoes, we all have a ball.

Hats on heads that look quite askew,
We dance around like we're brand new.
Frosty breath in the chilly air,
We giggle and bounce without a care.

Thick mittens hide our little tricks,
Snowballs fly, oh, what a mix!
My scarf's a snake that's lost its way,
Wrangled like spaghetti in bright dismay.

As we sip cocoa, now is the time,
To make silly faces and chatter in rhyme.
Evening comes, but we're still awake,
Where friendships stick like a sweet frosty flake.

Chasing the Chill Away

Bundled up tight, I can hardly move,
A dance-off starts, we all find our groove.
A tumble here, a giggle there,
Who knew the sleigh had that much flair?

Hot chocolate spills on my favorite hat,
I'm a cocoa monster, imagine that!
With each sip, my cheeks grow round,
Like a squirrel stashing nuts from the ground.

The wind whistles tunes, a frosty song,
We whistle back, it won't be long.
Snowmen frolic with goofy grins,
Waving their carrot noses, let the fun begin!

Chasing the chill with laughter loud,
We rule the night, a jolly crowd.
A snowball fight turns into a hug,
Winter's antics, all snug as a bug.

Layers of Warmth and Whimsy

I've got a layer, oh what a sight,
A sweater with stripes that squeals delight.
I trip on my scarf, it's a winding snake,
The fashion police would surely break!

My socks are mismatched, a rainbow parade,
Dance like nobody cares I'm afraid.
With every wiggle, I shed a chill,
A jig in the snow, oh what a thrill!

A hat so fluffy, it flops and flares,
Fashion disaster? Who really cares?
We huddle closer, a medley of cheer,
In this cozy chaos, all hearts feel near.

With a dash of whimsy on icy nights,
We share goofy laughs and cheerful sights.
Layers of warmth are our secret delight,
In the grand winter play, everything feels right.

Silence Wrapped in Softness

Snow settles gently, a muffled sound,
But giggles bubble up all around.
I trip on my boots, fall flat on my face,
In this frozen ballet, I've lost my grace.

Stars twinkle softly, like winks of delight,
We chase silly shadows far into the night.
A gentle whirl through the drifts we go,
Creating soft laughter as we tumble in snow.

Blankets piled high, we gather in cheer,
With stories and secrets, we hold them dear.
Each silly tale wrapped in warmth and glee,
In this wondrous wonderland, we're wild and free.

As the moon shines bright, our joy is uncontained,
In this soft embrace, all worries unchained.
Silence whispers softly, but joy rings clear,
Together in winter, with friends we hold near.

Winter's Tender Hug

A frosty breeze nips at my toes,
Yet here I stand in heavy clothes.
My scarf's a creature, alive and grand,
It swallows me whole—I'm a woolly brand.

The gloves wave hello, as snowflakes fall,
In this fluffy fortress, I can't feel at all.
I trip on my mitten, take a clumsy dive,
In the land of the cozy, I feel so alive!

Each hat on my head, it's a woolly crown,
With every style pulling me down.
I tumble and giggle, it's quite the scene,
In this winter wonderland, I'm a fuzzy machine!

So let the cold come, let the chill bite,
For in my wool cocoon, I'm feeling just right.
With laughter and warmth, I'll dance in the snow,
In my fluffy attire, I'm ready to go!

The Softest Armor

In layers so thick, I can't even bend,
I'm a soft pillow, not quite a friend.
My sweater's a fortress, oh what a sight,
With buttons like shields, I'm ready to fight!

The beanie sits snug, a woolen hat knight,
It claims that it's fashion, but oh, what a fright!
With pom-poms and tassels, I wobble around,
Like a walking plush toy, I'm lost, never found.

My boots are so furry, they're begging to dance,
But tripping on laces ruins my chance.
In this fluffy chaos, I chuckle and spin,
While the snowflakes whisper, "Let winter begin!"

With laughter and warmth, I'll dance through the day,
In my softest armor, come join me, hooray!
So raise a warm cup, let's toast to the fun,
In this cuddly chaos, we've already won!

Wrapped in Nature's Embrace

I step outside, snug as a bug,
In this fluffy speak, I can't even shrug.
The world is a canvas of white and blue,
While I roll in the snow, like a giant chew toy too!

Snowflakes are dancing, a cold little kiss,
Yet my woolly cocoon makes me feel like bliss.
I pull on my mittens, they scatter about,
A one-man band, I can't sing, just shout!

I launch a snowball, it lands with a splat,
My hat takes a tumble—where's the cat?
With laughter erupting, it's a snowy buffet,
We feast on the fun, until the end of the day!

In nature's embrace, I chuckle and twirl,
Wooly and wobbly, let my laughter unfurl.
So immerse in this whimsy, let's share the delight,
In this wintery chaos, we'll dance through the night!

Beneath the Spiral of Frost

In a frosty maze where giggles abound,
I'm lost in my layers, like a giant round mound.
With each twirling flake, I spin out of sight,
Beneath the spirals of frost, what a comical plight!

My nose is a cherry, my cheeks rubbed in frost,
Who knew being cozy could feel like I'm lost?
I tumble on ice, a slip and a slide,
In a woolly ensemble, can't swallow my pride!

The scarves start a dance, they flutter and flow,
Like fairytale ribbons, in the chill of the snow.
With laughter erupting, I wave them around,
In this frozen ballet, I'm whimsy unbound!

So let's raise our voices in a woolly cheer,
For the joy of the cold, let's spread holiday cheer!
Beneath the spiral of frost, let's warm up the air,
In this winter hilarity, I'll always be there!

Snuggle Up Beneath Winter's Gaze

Fuzzy hats and scratchy socks,
Snowflakes fall with icy knocks.
Cuddled up on the couch so wide,
With a cup of cocoa by my side.

Socks that don't quite fit my feet,
Fluffy mittens, oh what a treat.
But when I sneeze, oh what a sight,
A puff of fluff takes off in flight.

Blankets piled up, snowdrifts high,
Trying not to let my coffee dry.
The cat curls up, all wrapped in lace,
Stealing warmth in this cozy space.

Laughter echoes with each slip,
As I tumble and start to trip.
But every fall's a goofy cheer,
We laugh and snuggle, winter's here!

Interwoven Dreams of the Season

A scarf that's knitted much too long,
Hats adorned with a silly song.
My grandma's secrets tucked within,
Each stitch a giggle, where to begin?

Woolly jumpers with colors bright,
Look like a rainbow on a night.
Each snag a story, each loop a grin,
Fashion faux pas? Oh, just dive in!

Fluffy slippers, mismatched and bold,
With every step, a tale retold.
Slipping, sliding, down the hall,
Chasing my thoughts as my socks do fall.

In this tangle of knit and purl,
There's joy in chaos, like a whirl.
The warmth of laughter fills the air,
In our winter wonderland, we share!

Sanctuary of Frosted Texture

A fortress made of woolly dreams,
Where laughter bounces, joy redeems.
Each thread a hug, each color a cheer,
Creating warmth with everyone near.

Snowflakes dance outside my door,
While inside I can't take any more.
Of tangled yarn and countless balls,
I trip on stitches, and laughter calls.

Tangled up in cozy delight,
Hats flying off in our playful fight.
A race to the fridge for marshmallow fluff,
Not one of us can ever get enough.

Giggles echo through the thick wool,
A sanctuary where we all feel full.
This frosty texture, a playful snare,
In our whimsical world, we all share.

The Gathering of Fluffy Threads

Gather round, it's knitting time,
With needles clicking, oh so sublime.
From purl to knit, we weave our cheer,
Each goofy moment, bringing us near.

A ball of yarn rolls under the chair,
Socks should fit, but they just flare.
Where did the stitches go aflutter?
Lost in a laughter, a yarn-filled shutter.

Under the lights, we spin and twirl,
As winter's chill gives a gentle whirl.
With fuzzy hats and knotted spree,
Our handiwork like a great big sea.

So here we sit, a crafty brood,
Surrounded by wool, in a merry mood.
In the gathering glow, we find our zest,
Among fluffy threads, we feel the best!

The Tender Touch of Woolen Layers

In a sweater, too tight, I've become a ball,
I waddle like a penguin, and I can't stand tall.
My arms are like sausages, trapped in a sleeve,
I breathe in and out, oh, will I ever leave?

The hat on my head, it's stuffed like a bear,
With pom-poms and knitting, it pulls at my hair.
A scarf wraps around me, I can barely see,
I trip on my toes, it's a winter spree!

Each glove is a puzzle, five pieces to find,
They make my hands clumsy, while I'm in a bind.
I reach for my coffee, it spills on my coat,
At least I'm warm, be it a lopsided float!

As I dance in my gear, I'm the jester of snow,
With layers a-plenty, I steal the show!
But in all of this fluff, I wear winter pride,
Clothing me up, it's a fun frosty ride!

Soft Whispers in the Cold

When I venture outside, it's a blanket affair,
With layers of wool, oh, I'm wrapped like a chair.
Each step's like a shuffle, my shoes squeak with grace,
Like a turtle on ice, that's my winter place.

The mittens are cozy but stiff like a board,
I can't grab my phone; can winter be ignored?
A puff of my breath hangs like clouds on a string,
Maybe it's time to give up on this thing.

My chin's tucked away, just a nose peeps out,
I guess I'm still cute, though a little stout.
With cheeks rosy red and a giggle so bright,
I'm the silly marshmallow that bounces in light!

As snowflakes descend, I start to dance,
In fluffy oversized boots, I grin at the chance.
Winter might tease, but I'm here for the play,
With laughter a-plenty, make a snowman today!

Cozy Heartbeats in the Frost

In my woolly cocoon, I wiggle with glee,
Like a sausage in casing, how silly can we be?
Hot cocoa in hand, with marshmallows on top,
In this frosty wonderland, it's the best way to hop!

The frozen air bites, but I'm snug as can be,
My cheeks all a-blush, like a silly red bee.
I trip on the ice, and I tumble around,
But laughter erupts like a joyful sweet sound.

Each layer I wear is a hug from my mom,
With mittens and hats, I'm a soft, sweet pom-pom.
Snowmen are chuckling, as I flail in delight,
Winter is goofy, especially tonight!

As my breath draws a fog, I'm a ghost in the chill,
Woolen enchantments keep me warm, what a thrill!
So here's to the laughter, the warmth, and the cheer,
In a world wrapped in layers, we dance without fear!

Meeting the Chill in Softness

In the chill of the morning, I fluff up my coat,
I pull on my socks, they've devoured my toes.
With layers and layers, I look like a stack,
A walking, talking, wooly attack!

Each puff of my jacket inflates like a prize,
With my cheeks like red apples, I'm full of surprise.
The snowflakes are falling, I laugh at the show,
While I sway like a snowman, oh how I glow!

I tumble in snow, like a plump little ball,
My friends shout with laughter as I take a fall.
With my butt in the snow and my feet in the air,
Who knew winter's fun could be such a dare?

Yet with all of this fluff, joy sparks in the breeze,
In a world made of flannel, I'm fussy but pleased.
So bring on the cold, and let snowflakes ignite,
In the dance of the season, my heart feels just right!

Milton Keynes UK
Ingram Content Group UK Ltd.
UKHW030750121124
451094UK00013B/798